SOPHIA FAIRVIEW

Micro Plastic – Mega Consequences

Small Particles, Big Problems: The Microplastic Crisis Unveiled – An In-Depth Exploration of the Unseen Threats Lurking in Our Oceans, Soil, and Air.

First edition

ISBN: 9798223343844

This book was professionally typeset on Reedsy.
Find out more at reedsy.com

Contents

Preface

In an era where our planet faces unprecedented environmental challenges, the issue of microplastic pollution stands as a silent yet pervasive threat to the ecological balance we strive to maintain. "Micro Plastic: Mega Consequences" is more than a book; it is a clarion call to action, a deep dive into the invisible crisis that is unfolding in the waters of our world and beyond.

As we navigate the chapters of this book, we will explore the multifaceted nature of microplastic pollution – its origins, its insidious journey through our ecosystems, and the profound impact it has on both the environment and human health. This journey is not just about understanding the science behind microplastics but also about grasping the socio-economic and political dimensions that drive and complicate this global issue.

This book aims to bridge the gap between scientific research and public awareness, translating complex data into an accessible narrative that not only informs but also empowers. It is a narrative that underscores the interconnectedness of our actions and the environment we are part of, compelling us to rethink our relationship with plastic – a material so ingrained in our daily lives.

"Micro Plastic: Mega Consequences" is a testament to the power of collective effort. It brings together the voices of scientists, policymakers, industry leaders, and activists, weaving a comprehensive picture of the challenges we face and the solutions that lie within our reach. This is not just a story of despair but one of hope and possibility – a call to envision a future where sustainability is not just an ideal but a lived reality.

As you turn these pages, I invite you to join me in this critical conversation about our planet's health and our responsibility towards it. Let this book be a starting point for change – a change that begins with awareness, leads to action, and culminates in a world that respects and preserves the intricate beauty of its natural systems.

Together, let's embark on this vital journey towards understanding, responsibility, and action.

Warm regards,

Sophia Fairview

1

Introduction

In the vast realm of environmental concerns, few issues have gained as much recognition and urgency as the pervasive presence of microplastics. These minuscule plastic particles, measuring less than 5mm in size, have silently infiltrated our ecosystems, oceans, and even our bodies, raising profound questions about their origins, impacts, and potential solutions.

This book is a dedicated exploration of the microplastic conundrum. It seeks to provide clarity on the multifaceted issue of microplastics by delving into the fundamental aspects that define it. Our journey begins with a clear definition of what microplastics are and an exploration of their significance in the broader context of environmental conservation and human health.

The primary goal of this book is to analyze the microplastic problem comprehensively. We aim to provide you, the reader, with a deep understanding of the subject matter, supported by rigorous research and evidence. Alongside this understanding, we will explore potential solutions and strategies to address the challenges posed by microplastic pollution.

In the chapters that follow, we will embark on a journey through the world of microplastics, covering topics such as their origins, distribution in the environment, and their use in various industries. We will examine the far-reaching consequences of microplastics on both the environment and living organisms, including humans.

Furthermore, we will delve into the public perception of microplastics, the role of media coverage, and the legal regulations and guidelines that aim to mitigate their impact. We will also scrutinize the efforts of international and national organizations in addressing this issue and discuss the successes and obstacles they have encountered.

The responsibility of industries and businesses in adopting sustainable practices and reducing microplastic emissions will be a significant focus. Additionally, we will highlight the pivotal role of local initiatives, educational programs, and activism in raising awareness and driving positive change.

Technological advancements and innovative solutions for microplastic removal will also be explored, providing insights into the tools and strategies available to combat this global problem.

As we navigate through these chapters, we will keep an eye on the future, examining emerging challenges, technological developments, and areas where further research is needed. Our ultimate aim is to provide you with a comprehensive resource that not only educates but also inspires action to address the microplastic predicament.

Thank you for joining us on this enlightening journey as we unravel the complexities of microplastics and explore the path forward toward a cleaner and healthier environment.

2

Definition of Microplastics

Microplastics, the focal point of our inquiry, are minute plastic particles that measure less than 5 millimeters in diameter. These diminutive fragments can take various forms, encompassing microbeads used in personal care products, microfibers shed from textiles, and fragments derived from the breakdown of larger plastic items.

The classification of microplastics is further refined based on their size:

1. **Primary Microplastics:** These are manufactured as small particles for specific purposes. Primary microplastics include microbeads in exfoliating scrubs and abrasive cleaning products, as well as the tiny plastic pellets used in industrial processes.

2. **Secondary Microplastics:** Secondary microplastics originate from the breakdown of larger plastic items, such as plastic bottles, bags, and fishing nets. Over time, exposure to environmental factors like sunlight and water causes

these items to fragment into smaller particles.

Microplastics pose a unique challenge because of their size and persistence. They are small enough to be ingested by a wide range of organisms, from plankton to larger marine animals, and can enter the food chain, potentially reaching humans. Their persistence in the environment means that once released, they can persist for decades, contributing to long-term pollution.

Significance of Microplastic Pollution

The significance of microplastic pollution cannot be overstated, as it represents a multifaceted challenge with far-reaching implications for both the environment and human health. Here, we delve into the key aspects that underscore the importance of addressing this issue:

1. **Environmental Impact:** Microplastics have infiltrated ecosystems worldwide, from the depths of the oceans to remote wilderness areas. They pose a direct threat to aquatic life, as marine organisms mistakenly ingest these tiny particles, leading to physical harm, altered feeding behaviors, and even death. The persistence of microplastics in the environment disrupts natural ecosystems and can have cascading effects on food chains.
2. **Human Health Concerns:** Research has shown that microplastics are not confined to marine environments; they have been found in the air we breathe, the water we drink, and the food we consume. The potential health

risks associated with microplastic ingestion or inhalation are still being studied but may include inflammation, oxidative stress, and the transfer of harmful chemicals. Understanding and mitigating these risks are paramount for safeguarding public health.

3. **Global Scope:** Microplastic pollution is a global issue, transcending geographical boundaries. It necessitates international collaboration and concerted efforts to address its origins and impacts effectively. The interconnectedness of ecosystems means that actions taken in one part of the world can have consequences far beyond their immediate location.

4. **Economic Costs:** Beyond the environmental and health concerns, microplastic pollution carries economic burdens. Cleaning up microplastics from beaches, water bodies, and treatment facilities is costly. Industries that rely on clean and healthy oceans, such as fisheries and tourism, can suffer due to microplastic contamination.

5. **Long-Term Consequences:** Microplastics' persistence in the environment means that their effects may linger for decades or even centuries. As we continue to produce and release plastic into the environment, the problem of microplastic pollution is likely to worsen unless proactive measures are taken.

6. **Public Awareness:** The growing awareness of microplastic pollution among the general public and the media has amplified the urgency of addressing this issue. Individuals and communities are demanding action, pressuring industries and governments to adopt more sustainable practices and regulations.

3

Purpose of the Book

Analyzing the Microplastic Issue and Exploring Solutions

The overarching purpose of this book is twofold: to provide a comprehensive analysis of the microplastic problem and to offer insights into potential solutions. This dual objective is rooted in the recognition of the complexity and urgency surrounding microplastic pollution.

1. **Comprehensive Analysis:** The book aims to offer readers a thorough and well-researched understanding of microplastics from various angles. We intend to dissect the issue, exploring its origins, distribution, environmental impact, and consequences for human health. Through rigorous research and clear explanations, our goal is to equip readers with a deep knowledge of this multifaceted problem.

2. **Exploration of Solutions:** Beyond analysis, the book will delve into potential solutions to address the microplastic challenge. This includes examining existing and emerging

technologies for microplastic removal, considering the roles of industries and governments in mitigating pollution, and highlighting the significance of grassroots initiatives and public awareness campaigns. We aim to provide a balanced view of the diverse strategies available to combat microplastic pollution.

3. **Facilitating Informed Action:** By presenting a well-rounded perspective on microplastics and their impacts, the book empowers readers to make informed decisions and take action. Whether you are an environmental advocate, policymaker, industry professional, or concerned citizen, the insights within these pages can serve as a valuable resource for driving positive change.

4. **Promoting Collaboration:** Microplastic pollution is a global challenge that requires collaboration across borders, disciplines, and sectors. This book encourages readers to think critically about the issue and consider how their own actions and spheres of influence can contribute to the collective effort to combat microplastic pollution.

Ultimately, our aim is not only to inform but also to inspire. We believe that by comprehensively understanding the microplastic problem and exploring a spectrum of solutions, we can work together to mitigate its impact and forge a more sustainable future.

As we progress through the chapters, we invite you to engage actively with the material, reflect on the implications, and join us in our quest to address the microplastic predicament.

4

Microplastics: Understanding and Identification

I n Part II of this book, we venture deeper into the intricate world of microplastics, focusing on understanding their origins, distribution, and the methods employed to identify these tiny yet pervasive particles. This section is dedicated to shedding light on the scientific aspects of microplastics and their implications for our environment and health.

Our journey begins with a closer look at the sources and pathways through which microplastics enter the environment. We will explore the various industries that use microplastics and their contribution to the issue. Additionally, we'll delve into the intricate web of interactions between microplastics and the living organisms that encounter them.

This section is an essential foundation for comprehending the broader picture of microplastics' impact on our planet. By understanding their origins and behaviors, we can better appreciate the challenges they pose and the urgency of addressing this issue.

Origin and Distribution of Microplastics in the Environment

Understanding the origin and distribution of microplastics is crucial to grasp the extent of this pervasive environmental issue. In this section, we will explore how these tiny plastic particles find their way into the environment and the pathways they take to become ubiquitous.

1. **Natural Breakdown:** One significant source of microplastics in the environment is the breakdown of larger plastic items. Over time, exposure to sunlight, wind, and water causes plastics such as bottles, bags, and fishing nets to degrade into smaller particles. These secondary microplastics are released into the environment, where they can persist for extended periods.

2. **Microbeads in Personal Care Products:** Microplastics are intentionally added to a range of personal care products like exfoliating scrubs and toothpaste as microbeads. When these products are used and washed off, the microbeads are often too small to be effectively filtered out in wastewater treatment plants. Consequently, they can end up in rivers, lakes, and oceans.

3. **Microfibers from Textiles:** Another significant source of microplastics is the shedding of microfibers from synthetic textiles during washing. These tiny plastic threads are released from clothing made of materials like polyester and nylon and are carried through sewage systems into natural water bodies.

4. **Industrial Processes:** Microplastics are used in various industrial processes, such as abrasive blasting and as carriers for chemicals in agriculture. During these processes, microplastics can be released into the environment, contributing to pollution.

5. **Atmospheric Deposition:** Surprisingly, microplastics

have been found in the air we breathe. They can become airborne through processes like tire wear, road abrasion, and the breakdown of plastic litter. These particles eventually settle back to the ground or may be carried by winds over long distances.

6. **Runoff from Urban Areas:** Urban runoff, including stormwater, can transport microplastics from streets and other urban surfaces into water bodies, further distributing them in the environment.

7. **Marine Discharges:** The shipping industry, through activities like bilge water discharge and the loss of cargo, can also introduce microplastics into marine environments.

Use of Microplastics in Various Industries

Microplastics find their way into the environment through intentional use in various industrial processes and products. In this section, we will explore the different industries where microplastics are employed and the reasons behind their utilization.

1. **Cosmetics and Personal Care Products:** One of the most widely recognized uses of microplastics is in cosmetics and personal care items. Microbeads, small plastic particles, have historically been added to products like exfoliating scrubs, shower gels, and toothpaste for their abrasive properties. These microbeads can end up in the environment when products are washed down the drain.

2. **Textile Industry:** The textile industry contributes significantly to microplastic pollution. Synthetic fabrics like polyester, nylon, and acrylic release microfibers during washing and wear. These microfibers are small enough to escape filtration systems in wastewater treatment plants and are discharged into water

bodies.

3. Industrial Abrasives: Microplastics, particularly in the form of tiny plastic beads, are used in industrial applications as abrasives. They are employed in processes like sandblasting and grinding due to their abrasive properties.

4. Agriculture: In agriculture, microplastics can be used as carriers for pesticides and fertilizers. They serve as a delivery mechanism for these chemicals, but their release into the environment can contribute to pollution.

5. Packaging Materials: Microplastics can find their way into the environment through packaging materials. For instance, some plastic films used in packaging can break down into smaller particles over time.

6. Manufacturing Processes: Microplastics may be used in manufacturing processes where they serve specific purposes. For example, they can be added to paint to improve its texture or as a filler material in various products.

7. Construction: In the construction industry, microplastics can be found in products like paints, coatings, and sealants, where they are used to enhance performance characteristics.

Health Impacts on Humans and Wildlife

Microplastic pollution has raised concerns about its potential health impacts on both human beings and wildlife. In this section, we will delve into the growing body of research that examines how microplastics can affect living organisms.

1. Ingestion: One of the primary concerns is the ingestion of microplastics by various species. Marine organisms, such as fish and shellfish, can mistake microplastics for food particles and ingest them. This ingestion can lead to physical harm, blockages in digestive systems, and malnutrition, ultimately affecting the overall health and survival of these organisms.

2. Bioaccumulation: Microplastics can enter the food chain when smaller organisms consume them, and larger predators consume those smaller organisms. This process can lead to the bioaccumulation of microplastics in higher trophic levels, potentially posing a risk to human consumers of seafood.

3. Chemical Contamination: Microplastics have a unique capacity to absorb and accumulate chemical pollutants from the surrounding environment. When ingested, these chemicals can leach from the microplastics into the bodies of organisms, potentially causing toxicity and adverse health effects.

4. Disruption of Biological Functions: Research suggests that microplastics can disrupt various biological functions in organisms. This disruption can manifest as inflammation, oxidative stress, changes in feeding behavior, reproductive issues, and altered immune responses.

5. Transfer to Humans: Microplastics have been detected in various human tissues and organs, including the gastrointestinal tract. While the health implications of this presence are still under investigation, it raises concerns about the potential for humans to be exposed to microplastics through their diet and the environment.

6. Inhalation: Microplastics have been found in the air, leading to concerns about their inhalation by humans. This may be particularly relevant in urban areas and industries where airborne microplastics are generated.

5

Environmental Impacts and Public Perception

In Part III of our exploration of microplastics, we venture into the intricate realms of environmental consequences and the role of public perception in addressing this pervasive issue. This section delves into the profound impact of microplastics on ecosystems and the growing awareness of their presence among the general public.

Environmental Impacts:

Our journey begins with a closer examination of how microplastics affect the environment. We will unravel the intricate web of interactions between these tiny plastic particles and the ecosystems they infiltrate. From the depths of the oceans to the pristine wilderness, we will uncover the far-reaching consequences of microplastic pollution.

We will explore how microplastics disrupt natural habitats, enter food chains, and pose threats to aquatic and terrestrial life. Our aim is to provide a comprehensive understanding of the ecological toll exacted by these minuscule invaders and the urgency of mitigating their impact.

Public Perception and Awareness:

The second facet of Part III delves into the role of public perception, media coverage, and the growing awareness of microplastics. In an age of instant information and global communication, the public's perception of environmental issues plays a pivotal role in shaping policies, regulations, and industry practices.

We will explore how the media portrays microplastics, the impact of visual narratives, and the power of storytelling in conveying the urgency of this issue. Moreover, we will examine how public awareness can translate into collective action, influencing consumer choices, industry practices, and political decisions.

Effects of Microplastics on the Environment

Microplastics, despite their small size, have profound and far-reaching consequences on the environment. In this section, we will delve into the specific impacts of microplastics on our ecosystems, highlighting the intricate web of interactions and consequences they engender.

1. **Marine Ecosystems:** Microplastics pose a significant threat to marine life. They can be ingested by a wide range of organisms, including plankton, fish, and marine mammals. This ingestion can lead to physical harm, malnutrition, and reduced reproductive success. Microplastics can also disrupt the behavior and feeding patterns of marine species, potentially altering entire food webs.

2. Terrestrial Ecosystems: Microplastics are not confined to aquatic environments. They have been found in soils, posing potential risks to terrestrial organisms and ecosystems. Their presence in soils can affect nutrient cycling and microbial communities, with cascading effects on plant health and ecosystem dynamics.

3. Freshwater Ecosystems: Microplastics can also enter freshwater ecosystems through various routes, including runoff from urban areas and wastewater discharge. In freshwater environments, they can accumulate and impact aquatic life, similar to their effects in marine ecosystems.

4. Bioaccumulation and Biomagnification: Microplastics have the potential to bioaccumulate in organisms, meaning that they can build up in an organism's tissues over time. This bioaccumulation is particularly concerning when it occurs in species higher up the food chain, as it can lead to biomagnification, where the concentration of microplastics increases at each trophic level.

5. Habitat Alteration: The accumulation of microplastics in sediments and habitats can alter the physical structure of ecosystems. This can affect the availability of natural habitats and influence the distribution and behavior of species.

6. Chemical Contamination: Microplastics can absorb and release chemicals from the surrounding environment. This can include pollutants like pesticides and heavy metals, potentially leading to toxic effects on organisms that come into contact with microplastics.

7. Long-Term Environmental Persistence: One of the significant challenges of microplastics is their long-term persistence in the environment. Once released, they can remain for decades or even centuries, continually affecting ecosystems.

Public Perception, Media Coverage, and Awareness

Public perception and media coverage play pivotal roles in shaping how society responds to environmental issues like microplastic pollution. In this section, we will delve into the evolving landscape of public awareness, the influence of media narratives, and the power of information dissemination.

1. Media's Role in Shaping Perception: Media outlets, including news organizations, documentaries, and online platforms, have a significant influence on how microplastic pollution is portrayed to the public. Investigative reporting, visual storytelling, and documentaries have brought the issue to the forefront of public awareness. We will explore how media coverage can spark public interest and influence attitudes and behaviors.

2. Visual Impact: Visual narratives, such as images of marine life entangled in plastic debris or seabirds with stomachs full of plastic, can be particularly powerful in conveying the urgency of the issue. These images evoke emotional responses and can drive individuals, organizations, and governments to take action.

3. Awareness Campaigns: Environmental organizations, non-governmental organizations (NGOs), and concerned individuals have launched awareness campaigns to educate the public about microplastic pollution. These campaigns often leverage social media, online platforms, and public events to engage and mobilize communities.

4. Policy and Regulation: Public awareness and concern about microplastics have led to increased pressure on governments and industries to address the issue. This has resulted in the development of policies, regulations, and bans on certain microplastic products in various regions.

5. Consumer Choices: As public awareness has grown, consumers have become more conscientious about their choices, including the products they purchase and their consumption habits. This shift in consumer behavior can influence market demand and drive industries to adopt more sustainable practices.

6. Citizen Science: Public engagement in citizen science initiatives has contributed to data collection efforts related to microplastics. Individuals and communities actively participate in monitoring and research, adding valuable information to the scientific understanding of the issue.

7. Challenges and Misconceptions: Despite increased awareness, there are still challenges and misconceptions surrounding microplastic pollution. Some segments of the public may not fully grasp the scope of the problem or its potential health and environmental impacts.

Legal Regulations and Regulations

The regulation of microplastics is an essential aspect of addressing the pervasive issue of microplastic pollution. In this section, we will explore the role of legal regulations and guidelines in mitigating the impact of microplastics on the environment and human health.

1. International Agreements and Treaties: Various international agreements and treaties have been established to address marine pollution, including microplastics. For example, the MARPOL Annex V regulates the discharge of garbage, including plastics, from ships into the sea. These agreements promote international cooperation in reducing plastic pollution in oceans.

2. National Legislation: Many countries have introduced

national legislation and regulations aimed at curbing microplastic pollution. These measures may include bans on certain microplastic products, restrictions on their use in manufacturing, and requirements for labeling.

3. Microbead Bans: Some regions have implemented specific bans on microbeads in personal care products. These bans restrict the use of microbeads in items like exfoliating scrubs, toothpaste, and cosmetics.

4. Extended Producer Responsibility (EPR): In some jurisdictions, EPR programs have been introduced to hold manufacturers responsible for the end-of-life management of their plastic products, including microplastics. This can incentivize producers to adopt more sustainable materials and practices.

5. Monitoring and Reporting Requirements: Some regulations require industries to monitor and report on their microplastic emissions. This can include assessments of microplastic levels in products, emissions into the environment, and measures to reduce these emissions.

6. Research Funding: Governments may allocate research funding to better understand microplastic pollution and its impacts. This research informs policy decisions and contributes to evidence-based regulations.

7. Public Advocacy: Public pressure and advocacy from environmental organizations and concerned citizens play a crucial role in driving legislative changes. Public support can lead to the introduction and passage of regulations aimed at curbing microplastic pollution.

8. Challenges and Enforcement: While regulations are essential, challenges often arise in enforcing them effectively. Monitoring compliance and ensuring that industries adhere to regulations can be complex and resource-intensive.

6

Microplastics in the Ocean Environment

Microplastics pose significant threats to the ocean environment, affecting marine life, ecosystems, and even human activities. In this section, we will explore the consequences of microplastic pollution in the oceans.

The Journey of Microplastics to the Ocean: Microplastics enter the ocean through various pathways, including runoff from urban areas, industrial discharges, and coastal activities. Wind can also transport microplastics from land to sea. Once in the ocean, these tiny plastic particles can travel vast distances and persist for a long time.

Pathways to the Ocean: How Microplastics Travel from Land to Sea: Microplastics are transported to the ocean through several routes:

- **Stormwater Runoff:** Rainwater washes microplastics from streets, sidewalks, and other urban surfaces into storm drains, eventually reaching rivers and oceans.
- **Wastewater Discharges:** Microplastics from household

products, including personal care items and detergents, can pass through wastewater treatment plants and enter water bodies.

- **Rivers and Waterways:** Rivers act as conduits for microplastics from inland areas to coastal regions. Large rivers, in particular, can transport significant amounts of microplastics.
- **Marine Activities:** Activities such as shipping, fishing, and recreational boating can introduce microplastics directly into the ocean.

Role of Rivers and Waterways: Their Part in Transporting Microplastics: Rivers and waterways play a crucial role in transporting microplastics from land to the ocean. As rivers flow through urban and industrial areas, they accumulate microplastics from runoff and discharges. When these rivers reach the coast, they release microplastics into marine environments. Coastal areas, where many marine species breed and feed, become hotspots for microplastic contamination.

Accumulation Zones: Identifying Areas with High Concentrations of Microplastics: Several ocean regions have been identified as accumulation zones for microplastics. These areas are often characterized by ocean currents that trap and concentrate floating microplastics. The Great Pacific Garbage Patch is one such well-known accumulation zone.

Consequences for Marine Life and Ecosystems: Microplastics can have dire consequences for marine life. They are often mistaken for food by aquatic organisms, leading to ingestion and potential harm. When ingested, microplastics can block digestive tracts, cause physical damage, and leach toxic chemicals into the animals.

Microplastics can also accumulate in the food chain, potentially impacting larger predators, including fish and marine mammals. Furthermore, they can alter marine ecosystems, affecting the composition and behavior of various species.

Human Implications: Beyond their effects on marine life, microplastics may have indirect consequences for human health. When microplastic-contaminated seafood is consumed, there is the potential for humans to ingest these particles. While research is ongoing, concerns have been raised about the possible health risks associated with microplastic exposure.

The Consequences of Microplastics to the Ocean Environment

Microplastics pose significant threats to the ocean environment, affecting marine life, ecosystems, and even human activities. In this section, we will explore the consequences of microplastic pollution in the oceans.

The Journey of Microplastics to the Ocean: Microplastics enter the ocean through various pathways, including runoff from urban areas, industrial discharges, and coastal activities. Wind can also transport microplastics from land to sea. Once in the ocean, these tiny plastic particles can travel vast distances and persist for a long time.

Pathways to the Ocean: How Microplastics Travel from Land to Sea: Microplastics are transported to the ocean through several routes:

- **Stormwater Runoff:** Rainwater washes microplastics from streets, sidewalks, and other urban surfaces into storm drains, eventually reaching rivers and oceans.

- **Wastewater Discharges:** Microplastics from household products, including personal care items and detergents, can pass through wastewater treatment plants and enter water bodies.
- **Rivers and Waterways:** Rivers act as conduits for microplastics from inland areas to coastal regions. Large rivers, in particular, can transport significant amounts of microplastics.
- **Marine Activities:** Activities such as shipping, fishing, and recreational boating can introduce microplastics directly into the ocean.

Role of Rivers and Waterways: Their Part in Transporting Microplastics: Rivers and waterways play a crucial role in transporting microplastics from land to the ocean. As rivers flow through urban and industrial areas, they accumulate microplastics from runoff and discharges. When these rivers reach the coast, they release microplastics into marine environments. Coastal areas, where many marine species breed and feed, become hotspots for microplastic contamination.

Accumulation Zones: Identifying Areas with High Concentrations of Microplastics: Several ocean regions have been identified as accumulation zones for microplastics. These areas are often characterized by ocean currents that trap and concentrate floating microplastics. The Great Pacific Garbage Patch is one such well-known accumulation zone.

Consequences for Marine Life and Ecosystems: Microplastics can have dire consequences for marine life. They are often mistaken for food by aquatic organisms, leading to ingestion and potential harm. When ingested, microplastics can block digestive tracts, cause physical damage, and leach toxic chemicals into the animals.

Microplastics can also accumulate in the food chain, potentially impacting larger predators, including fish and marine mammals. Furthermore, they can alter marine ecosystems, affecting the composition and behavior of various species.

Human Implications: Beyond their effects on marine life, microplastics may have indirect consequences for human health. When microplastic-contaminated seafood is consumed, there is the potential for humans to ingest these particles. While research is ongoing, concerns have been raised about the possible health risks associated with microplastic exposure.

In conclusion, microplastic pollution in the ocean poses significant challenges to marine ecosystems, wildlife, and potentially human health. Understanding the pathways by which microplastics enter the ocean and their consequences is vital for developing effective strategies to mitigate this global environmental issue.

Impact on Marine Life

Microplastics pose a significant threat to marine life, with consequences ranging from ingestion to physical and chemical effects. In this section, we will explore how microplastics affect marine species.

Ingestion by Marine Species: How Microplastics are Consumed by Marine Animals:

Marine animals, from plankton to large predators, can ingest microplastics, often mistaking them for prey. This ingestion can occur through various mechanisms:

1. **Filter Feeding:** Filter-feeding organisms, such as bivalves

(mussels, clams) and some species of plankton, ingest microplastics when they filter tiny particles from the water. Microplastics suspended in the water column are inadvertently consumed along with phytoplankton and other particles.

2. **Predation:** Larger marine species, including fish, birds, and marine mammals, may consume microplastics when they ingest prey that has already ingested microplastics. This bioaccumulation of microplastics can occur through the food chain, with potential consequences for top predators.

3. **Direct Ingestion:** Some marine animals may directly ingest microplastics if they mistake them for food items. For example, sea turtles might ingest plastic bags, thinking they are jellyfish, while seabirds may consume small plastic fragments, mistaking them for fish or squid.

Physical and Chemical Effects: Analyzing the Impact on the Health and Behavior of Marine Species:

The impact of microplastics on marine species can manifest in several ways:

1. **Physical Damage:** Ingested microplastics can physically harm marine organisms. Larger particles can block digestive tracts, leading to reduced nutrient absorption and malnutrition. In some cases, the presence of microplastics can cause injury or abrasions to the digestive organs of marine animals.

2. **Toxic Effects:** Microplastics can carry adsorbed pollutants and chemicals from the surrounding environment. When

ingested, these chemicals can leach into the tissues of marine organisms, potentially causing toxic effects. This is of particular concern when microplastics transport persistent organic pollutants (POPs), which can accumulate in organisms over time.

3. **Altered Behavior:** Microplastic ingestion can alter the behavior of marine species. For example, fish that consume microplastics might exhibit changes in feeding behavior, reduced swimming speed, or impaired predator avoidance abilities. These alterations can have cascading effects on ecosystem dynamics.

4. **Bioaccumulation:** Microplastics can accumulate in the tissues of marine animals over time. As smaller organisms are ingested by larger ones, microplastics can biomagnify up the food chain, potentially impacting top predators. This bioaccumulation raises concerns about the effects on commercially important fish species and seafood safety.

5. **Reproductive Impacts:** Some studies suggest that exposure to microplastics may affect the reproduction and development of marine organisms. For example, endocrine-disrupting chemicals associated with microplastics could impact reproductive processes.

6. **Health Implications for Humans:** While research on the transfer of microplastics from marine organisms to humans is ongoing, there are concerns about the potential health risks associated with consuming seafood contaminated with microplastics.

1. Zooplankton and Phytoplankton:

- Researchers in the North Atlantic Ocean found that zooplankton were ingesting microplastics, which affected their feeding behavior and energy balance. This has potential repercussions for the entire marine food web, as zooplankton are a crucial food source for higher trophic levels.

2. Fish:

- A study conducted in the Mediterranean Sea revealed that several fish species, including commercially important ones, had ingested microplastics. The ingestion of microplastics can disrupt fish digestion, potentially leading to reduced growth and reproduction.

3. Sea Turtles:

- Sea turtles, such as loggerheads and green turtles, are known to ingest plastic debris, including microplastics. Ingested microplastics can block their digestive tracts and cause malnutrition. The presence of microplastics in the gastrointestinal tract can also lead to internal injuries.

4. Seabirds:

- Seabirds, like albatrosses and shearwaters, often mistake floating microplastics for prey items. This can lead to the ingestion of plastic particles, which can accumulate in their stomachs and reduce their food intake, potentially affecting their reproductive success.

5. Marine Mammals:

· Whales and dolphins, such as the sperm whale, have been found with plastic debris, including microplastics, in their stomachs. The ingestion of microplastics can lead to reduced feeding efficiency, malnutrition, and potential long-term health impacts on these marine mammals.

6. Coral Reefs:

· While not a marine organism, coral reefs are vital ecosystems. Microplastics can become entangled in corals, potentially harming their health. The presence of microplastics can also facilitate the growth of harmful pathogens that affect coral health.

7. Commercially Harvested Species:

· Commercially harvested species, such as oysters and mussels, have been found to contain microplastics. The ingestion of microplastics by these organisms raises concerns about the safety of seafood consumption and the potential transfer of microplastics to humans.

Habitat Alteration: How Microplastics Affect Coral Reefs and Other Vital Habitats:

Microplastics can have detrimental effects on marine habitats, including coral reefs, seagrass beds, and coastal ecosystems. Here's how microplastics impact these vital habitats:

1. **Coral Reefs:** Coral reefs are among the most biodiverse ecosystems on Earth, providing habitat for countless marine species. Microplastics can become entangled in corals,

leading to physical damage and impairing their ability to feed and reproduce. Additionally, microplastics can serve as a substrate for harmful pathogens, increasing the risk of coral diseases. The health of coral reefs is crucial not only for marine biodiversity but also for coastal protection and fisheries.

2. **Seagrass Beds:** Seagrass beds are important nursery grounds for many marine species. Microplastics can accumulate in seagrass habitats, potentially smothering seagrass shoots and reducing the availability of oxygen to seagrass roots. This disturbance can have cascading effects on the organisms that rely on seagrass habitats for shelter and food.

3. **Coastal Ecosystems:** Microplastics can contaminate coastal environments, including estuaries and marshes. These areas are critical for various species during different life stages. The presence of microplastics can disrupt the delicate balance of these ecosystems, affecting the growth and survival of organisms such as crabs, fish, and birds.

Long-Term Ecological Impacts: Potential Future Scenarios for Marine Ecosystems:

The long-term ecological impacts of microplastic pollution on marine ecosystems are a growing concern. Here are potential future scenarios for marine ecosystems:

1. **Biodiversity Loss:** Continued microplastic pollution could lead to the decline of certain species that are particularly vulnerable to ingestion or entanglement. This could result in reduced biodiversity and altered species compositions in marine ecosystems.

2. **Shifts in Trophic Structures:** Changes in the abundance and distribution of species within marine food webs may occur due to microplastic pollution. This can lead to shifts in trophic structures, with potential implications for the overall functioning of marine ecosystems.

3. **Ecosystem Services:** Marine ecosystems provide essential ecosystem services, including fisheries, coastal protection, and carbon sequestration. If microplastic pollution disrupts these ecosystems, it could have far-reaching consequences for human societies, affecting food security, coastal resilience, and climate regulation.

4. **Unknown Ecological Feedbacks:** The full extent of ecological feedbacks resulting from microplastic pollution is not yet fully understood. This uncertainty underscores the need for continued research to better grasp the complex interactions between microplastics and marine ecosystems.

The Importance of Ocean Health for Oxygen Production:

It's worth emphasizing that the health of the world's oceans is closely tied to the production of oxygen. Phytoplankton, microscopic marine plants, are responsible for a significant portion of the oxygen we breathe. These tiny organisms perform photosynthesis, producing oxygen as a byproduct.

If marine ecosystems, including phytoplankton populations, are compromised by factors like microplastic pollution and climate change, there is a risk that oxygen production could be negatively impacted. Ensuring the health and vitality of our oceans is not only crucial for marine life but also for maintaining the oxygen levels necessary for terrestrial life on Earth.

The Human Connection

Microplastic pollution in the oceans has direct and indirect consequences for human well-being, ranging from seafood contamination to economic impacts and cultural dimensions. In this section, we will explore the various ways in which microplastics are intertwined with the human connection to the marine environment.

1. Seafood and Human Health: Exploring the Implications of Microplastics in the Human Food Chain:

- **Seafood Contamination:** Microplastics have been detected in various seafood species, including fish, shellfish, and mollusks. When humans consume contaminated seafood, there is a potential for ingesting microplastics. While the health effects of microplastic ingestion are still being studied, there are concerns about the potential transfer of microplastics and associated chemicals to human tissues.

- **Health Research:** Research is ongoing to understand the health implications of microplastic exposure in humans. Potential risks include inflammation, tissue damage, and the transfer of harmful chemicals associated with microplastics. It is essential to continue studying these potential health impacts to inform seafood safety guidelines.

2. Economic Impacts: How Microplastic Pollution Affects Fisheries, Tourism, and Coastal Communities:

- **Fisheries:** Microplastic pollution can have economic consequences for the fishing industry. Contaminated fish and shellfish may face reduced market demand, impacting the livelihoods of fishermen and seafood businesses. Additionally, fisheries may incur additional costs for compliance with seafood safety regulations.

- **Tourism:** Coastal tourism is a significant source of income for many communities. The presence of microplastic pollution on beaches and in nearshore waters can deter tourists, affecting local economies. Clean-up efforts and the management of plastic waste can also strain tourism budgets.
- **Coastal Communities:** Coastal communities often depend on healthy marine ecosystems for their livelihoods. Reduced fish stocks, impacts on aquaculture, and disrupted coastal ecosystems can threaten the economic stability of these communities.

3. Cultural and Social Dimensions: The Broader Impact on Human Societies Reliant on Healthy Oceans:

- **Cultural Significance:** Oceans hold cultural significance for many societies. Coastal communities often have deep cultural connections to the sea, including traditions, practices, and rituals that revolve around marine environments. Microplastic pollution can disrupt these cultural bonds.
- **Social Equity:** Vulnerable and marginalized communities, particularly those in developing countries, may bear a disproportionate burden of microplastic pollution's impacts. These communities often have limited resources to address pollution and adapt to its consequences.
- **Global Interconnectedness:** Microplastic pollution is a global issue with interconnected consequences. Pollution in one part of the world can impact ecosystems and societies in distant regions through ocean currents and shared seafood

markets. Addressing microplastic pollution requires international cooperation.

Microplastics and Climate Change: Interactions with Greenhouse Gases

The relationship between microplastics and climate change is a complex one, involving both contributions to and mitigations of climate change. Here, we explore how microplastics interact with greenhouse gases and their potential impacts on climate.

1. Microplastic Emissions as a Source of Greenhouse Gases:

- **Methane Emissions:** Recent research has indicated that certain types of microplastics, particularly those found in the environment, can serve as hosts for methane-producing bacteria. Methane is a potent greenhouse gas. When microplastics provide a habitat for these methane-producing microorganisms, they can potentially increase methane emissions. This could contribute to enhanced greenhouse gas concentrations in the atmosphere.

2. Impact on Carbon Sequestration:

- **Carbon Sequestration:** Microplastics that sink to the ocean floor can interact with sediment and organic matter. In some cases, microplastics may alter sediment properties and microbial communities. These changes could affect the capacity of marine sediments to sequester carbon. A reduction in carbon sequestration potential could indirectly contribute to climate change by allowing more carbon dioxide to remain in the atmosphere.

3. Role in Mitigating Climate Change:

- **Carbon Capture Technologies:** Some research has explored the use of microplastics in carbon capture technologies. Specially designed microplastics with high surface areas could potentially be used to capture and store carbon dioxide emissions from industrial processes. While this concept is in its early stages, it suggests a potential role for microplastics in mitigating climate change.

4. Ecological and Environmental Context:

- It's essential to consider the broader ecological and environmental context of microplastic interactions with greenhouse gases. The effects of microplastics on methane emissions or carbon sequestration may vary depending on factors such as microplastic type, size, concentration, and the specific environmental conditions where they are found.

5. Overall Impact:

- The overall impact of microplastics on climate change is an emerging area of research. While microplastics may have some potential negative contributions to greenhouse gas emissions, it is crucial to emphasize that the primary driver of climate change remains the burning of fossil fuels and other human activities that release greenhouse gases into the atmosphere.

In summary, the relationship between microplastics and climate change is multifaceted. While some research suggests that microplastics may interact with methane-producing microorganisms and affect carbon sequestration, the extent of these effects and their significance in the context of global climate change is still an area of active investigation. Addressing the broader issue of microplastic pollution and its ecological impacts remains a critical component of environmental stewardship and climate change mitigation efforts.

7

Feedback Loops

Examining Complex Interactions Between Microplastic Pollution and Climate Dynamics

Microplastic pollution can engage in intricate feed-back loops with various climate dynamics, leading to both environmental and climatic consequences. In this section, we will explore some of these complex interactions.

1. Albedo Effect and Ocean Heating:

- **Albedo Effect:** Albedo refers to the reflectivity of Earth's surfaces. Light-colored surfaces, such as ice and snow, have high albedo and reflect solar radiation, contributing to cooling. Darker surfaces, like water, have low albedo and absorb heat. Microplastics can accumulate on the ocean surface, altering its reflectivity. When microplastics darken the ocean surface, it can reduce albedo, leading to increased absorption of solar energy and higher ocean temperatures.

- **Feedback Loop:** As the ocean warms due to reduced albedo, it can exacerbate the melting of polar ice and glaciers, further reducing Earth's overall albedo. This positive feedback loop can accelerate global warming and sea level rise.

2. Microplastic Transport and Climate-Driven Ocean Currents:

- **Ocean Currents:** Climate-driven changes in ocean currents, such as the slowing of the Atlantic Meridional Overturning Circulation (AMOC), can affect the distribution and transport of microplastics. These changes in ocean circulation patterns can influence where microplastics accumulate and impact coastal regions differently.
- **Feedback Loop:** Altered ocean currents driven by climate change can potentially redistribute microplastics, impacting the dispersal of pollutants and debris. In turn, microplastics can act as vectors for transporting pollutants, which can have ecological and climate-related consequences.

3. Carbon Cycling and Microplastic Interactions:

- **Microplastics in Sediments:** Microplastics that settle to the ocean floor can interact with sediments, potentially affecting carbon cycling processes. These interactions can alter sediment characteristics, microbial communities, and the breakdown of organic matter.
- **Feedback Loop:** Changes in carbon cycling and sediment processes due to microplastic interactions can influence the release of greenhouse gases, such as carbon dioxide

and methane, from marine sediments. These emissions can contribute to climate change, creating a feedback loop where microplastics indirectly impact climate dynamics.

4. Ocean Acidification and Microplastic Sorption:

- **Ocean Acidification:** The absorption of excess carbon dioxide by the oceans leads to ocean acidification, which can harm marine life, particularly calcifying organisms like corals and mollusks. Microplastics can sorb (absorb or adsorb) pollutants, including CO2.
- **Feedback Loop:** Microplastics with adsorbed CO2 may contribute to localized changes in seawater chemistry, potentially impacting ocean acidification in specific areas. The precise implications of this interaction on global ocean acidification trends require further study.

Predicting Future Trends: How Ongoing Climate Change Might Exacerbate the Microplastic Problem

Climate change and microplastic pollution are interconnected challenges that can mutually exacerbate each other. Here, we examine how ongoing climate change could worsen the microplastic problem in the future:

1. Increased Extreme Weather Events:

- **Climate Change Impact:** Climate change is leading to more frequent and intense extreme weather events, including storms, hurricanes, and heavy rainfall.
- **Microplastic Dispersal:** These extreme weather events can lead to the transport of microplastics from various sources (e.g., land, urban areas) into rivers, streams, and

eventually the ocean. Flooding and stormwater runoff can carry microplastics from terrestrial environments to aquatic ecosystems.

- **Exacerbation:** With more frequent and severe storms, the transport and distribution of microplastics could increase, potentially resulting in higher concentrations in marine environments.

2. Rising Sea Levels:

- **Climate Change Impact:** Rising sea levels are a consequence of global warming and can lead to coastal erosion and the inundation of coastal areas.
- **Microplastic Accumulation:** Coastal areas are often hotspots for microplastic accumulation due to the convergence of land-based sources and oceanic processes. Rising sea levels could inundate previously untouched microplastic deposits, releasing them back into the marine environment.
- **Exacerbation:** The re-release of previously buried microplastics could contribute to higher concentrations of microplastics in coastal waters, potentially affecting marine life and ecosystems.

3. Ocean Acidification and Microplastic Interaction:

- **Climate Change Impact:** Ocean acidification, driven by the absorption of excess carbon dioxide by the oceans, is affecting marine ecosystems.
- **Microplastic Sorption:** Microplastics can adsorb carbon dioxide and other pollutants from seawater.

- **Exacerbation:** As ocean acidification progresses, the altered seawater chemistry may influence the adsorption capacity of microplastics. Changes in microplastic behavior could affect their interactions with marine organisms and the transport of adsorbed chemicals.

4. Impacts on Marine Life:

- **Climate Change Impact:** Climate change can stress marine ecosystems, affecting the distribution and abundance of marine species.
- **Microplastic Ingestion:** Stressed or displaced marine species may exhibit altered feeding behaviors, potentially increasing their exposure to microplastics.
- **Exacerbation:** Changes in the behavior and distribution of marine species due to climate change could lead to increased ingestion of microplastics, potentially impacting the transfer of microplastics through marine food webs.

5. Feedback Loops with Carbon Cycling:

- **Climate Change Impact:** Climate change can alter carbon cycling processes in marine ecosystems.
- **Microplastic Interactions:** Microplastics settling into marine sediments can influence sediment characteristics and carbon cycling processes.
- **Exacerbation:** Climate-induced changes in sediment processes, combined with the presence of microplastics, may influence the release of greenhouse gases from marine sediments, contributing to climate change.

8

Global and National Policy Approaches

Part IV of our exploration delves into the critical realm of policy and governance in addressing the pervasive issue of microplastic pollution. This section focuses on the role of international and national policies, the impact of governmental initiatives, and the challenges in shaping effective strategies to combat microplastic pollution.

Global Policy Landscape:

Our journey begins with an examination of the global policy landscape. We will explore the roles and responsibilities of international organizations and agreements in addressing microplastic pollution. From the United Nations to regional bodies, we will unravel the mechanisms in place to foster international cooperation and coordination.

National Approaches:

We will then turn our attention to national approaches to microplastics. Different countries have developed diverse strategies, legislation, and regulations to tackle the issue within their borders. We will examine case studies and examples of how nations have approached microplastic pollution, highlighting successes and challenges.

Role of Governments:

Governments play a pivotal role in crafting policies and regulations that can have a profound impact on microplastic pollution. We will explore the responsibilities of governments at the federal, state, and local levels in implementing and enforcing measures to reduce microplastic emissions.

Challenges in Implementation:

Implementing effective policies and regulations can be challenging due to various factors, including industry interests, resource limitations, and enforcement issues. We will delve into the obstacles and complexities that governments face in translating policy into action.

Science-Policy Interface:

The interface between scientific research and policy formulation is a crucial aspect of addressing microplastic pollution. We will examine how scientific findings inform policy decisions and how policymakers navigate the wealth of research available on the topic.

Global Cooperation:

Microplastic pollution is a transboundary issue that requires global cooperation. We will explore collaborative initiatives among nations, regions, and international organizations aimed at collectively addressing the challenge of microplastic pollution.

As we navigate through the chapters of Part IV, we invite you to gain insights into the intricate interplay between policy, governance, and the pursuit of solutions to the microplastic predicament. Together, we will examine the pivotal role of governments and international cooperation in shaping a sustainable future in the face of this pervasive environmental challenge.

Role of International and National Organizations and Governments

The role of international and national organizations, as well as governments, is pivotal in addressing the complex issue of microplastic pollution. In this section, we will delve into how these entities contribute to efforts aimed at mitigating the impact of microplastics on the environment and human health.

1. International Organizations:
International organizations, such as the United Nations Environment Programme (UNEP) and the United Nations Development Programme (UNDP), play a critical role in fostering global cooperation and setting the agenda for addressing microplastic pollution. They facilitate discussions, coordinate research efforts, and promote the adoption of international agreements and guidelines.

2. Regional and Inter-Governmental Bodies:
Regional bodies, like the European Union (EU) and the Association of Southeast Asian Nations (ASEAN), often develop region-specific strategies and regulations to combat microplastic pollu-

tion. These organizations enable member states to collaborate on shared environmental challenges.

3. National Governments:

At the national level, governments play a central role in formulating policies, legislation, and regulations to address microplastic pollution within their territories. This includes initiatives to ban or restrict certain microplastic products, set emission standards, and establish monitoring and reporting requirements.

4. Research and Data Collection:

Governments and international organizations often fund and coordinate research efforts to better understand microplastic pollution. They support scientific studies, data collection, and monitoring programs to assess the extent of the issue and its impact on ecosystems and health.

5. Policy Development:

Both national and international entities engage in policy development to address microplastic pollution comprehensively. This involves crafting regulations, guidelines, and action plans that encompass aspects like microplastic usage, emissions reduction, waste management, and recycling.

6. Enforcement and Compliance:

Governments are responsible for enforcing the regulations and standards established to combat microplastic pollution. This includes monitoring industries for compliance, conducting inspections, and imposing penalties for violations.

7. Advocacy and Public Awareness:

National governments and international organizations often engage in advocacy efforts to raise public awareness about microplastic pollution. They work to educate the public, industries, and policymakers about the issue and its consequences.

8. Global Cooperation:

Microplastic pollution is a global challenge that transcends borders. International organizations and governments engage in collaborative initiatives, share best practices, and facilitate information exchange to foster global cooperation in addressing the issue.

Agreements, Treaties, and Legislation

Agreements, treaties, and legislation play a crucial role in addressing microplastic pollution at the international, regional, and national levels. In this section, we will delve into the key agreements, conventions, and laws that have been established to combat the pervasive issue of microplastics.

1. MARPOL Annex V: The International Convention for the Prevention of Pollution from Ships (MARPOL) Annex V addresses the discharge of garbage, including plastics, from ships into the sea. It includes regulations aimed at reducing marine litter, including microplastics, from vessels.

2. Basel Convention: The Basel Convention on the Control of Transboundary Movements of Hazardous Wastes and Their Disposal regulates the transboundary movement of hazardous wastes, including plastic waste. Amendments to the convention have included measures to address plastic waste, including microplastics.

3. Regional Agreements: Regional bodies, such as the European Union (EU), have adopted regulations to tackle microplastic pollution. The EU, for example, has banned certain single-use plastic products and set targets for reducing plastic waste.

4. National Legislation: Many countries have introduced national legislation and regulations to combat microplastic pollution. These can include bans on specific microplastic products, restrictions on their use in manufacturing, and requirements for labeling.

5. Plastic Waste Management Laws: Some nations have enacted comprehensive laws aimed at managing plastic waste, including provisions related to microplastics. These laws often address issues like recycling, waste collection, and extended producer responsibility.

6. Microbead Bans: Several countries and regions have implemented specific bans on microbeads in personal care products, restricting their use due to their contribution to microplastic pollution in aquatic environments.

7. Product Labeling: Legislation in some areas requires product labeling to inform consumers about the presence of microplastics in certain items, such as cosmetics and cleaning products.

8. Extended Producer Responsibility (EPR): EPR programs hold producers responsible for the end-of-life management of their plastic products, including microplastics. These programs aim to incentivize more sustainable materials and practices.

9. Monitoring and Reporting Requirements: Some regulations require industries to monitor and report on their microplastic emissions. This includes assessments of microplastic levels in products, emissions into the environment, and measures to reduce these emissions.

10. Ongoing Legislative Efforts: Legislation related to microplastics is continually evolving as the understanding of the issue deepens. Governments and lawmakers are actively considering and enacting new measures to address this environmental challenge.

The landscape of agreements, treaties, and legislation is dynamic, reflecting the growing recognition of the need to address microplastic pollution.

Successes and Challenges in Politics

Addressing microplastic pollution through political measures involves both successes and challenges. In this section, we will explore the achievements made in policy and governance to mitigate the impact of microplastics, as well as the ongoing challenges that policymakers and governments face.

Successes:

1. **International Agreements:** The MARPOL Annex V and the Basel Convention have made significant strides in regulating plastic waste, including microplastics, at the international level. These agreements promote cooperation among nations to reduce marine litter and control the transboundary movement of hazardous plastic waste.

2. **Regional Regulations:** Regional organizations, such as the European Union, have successfully implemented regulations to combat microplastic pollution. Measures like the ban on certain single-use plastic products and the establishment of recycling targets demonstrate regional commitment to addressing the issue.

3. **National Legislation:** Many countries have taken proactive steps to combat microplastic pollution by enacting national legislation. Bans on microbeads in personal care products, restrictions on single-use plastics, and extended producer responsibility (EPR) programs are examples of effective national measures.

4. **Public Awareness:** Political efforts to raise public awareness about microplastic pollution have yielded positive results. Increased awareness has driven changes in consumer behavior, encouraging individuals to make more sustainable choices and reduce plastic consumption.

Challenges:

1. **Enforcement:** One of the primary challenges in microplastic regulation is enforcement. Ensuring that industries adhere

to regulations and monitoring compliance can be resource-intensive and complex, particularly in global supply chains.

2. Data Gaps: There are still significant data gaps related to microplastics, including their sources, distribution, and long-term impacts. Policymakers often face challenges in making evidence-based decisions due to limited data.

3. Global Cooperation: While international agreements exist, achieving full global cooperation in addressing microplastic pollution remains a challenge. Differences in priorities, resources, and interests among nations can hinder effective collaboration.

4. Technological Solutions: Developing and implementing effective technologies for microplastic removal and monitoring pose challenges. Innovations are needed to tackle microplastic pollution comprehensively.

5. Plastic Production: The sheer scale of global plastic production remains a challenge. Efforts to reduce microplastics must address the root causes, including the production and consumption of plastic materials.

6. Consumer Behavior: Changing consumer behavior and reducing plastic consumption at the individual level is a complex challenge. Efforts to promote sustainable choices require continued education and incentives.

7. Emerging Microplastics: As new forms of microplastics, such as nanoplastics, are identified, policymakers face the challenge of regulating these emerging pollutants effectively.

9

Industry and Corporate Responsibility

art V of our exploration delves into the pivotal role of industry and corporate responsibility in addressing the pressing issue of microplastic pollution. In this section, we will navigate the landscape of businesses, manufacturers, and production processes, emphasizing their impact on microplastic emissions and their potential for sustainable change.

Industry Practices:

Our journey begins with a critical examination of industry practices related to microplastics. We will explore how various sectors, from cosmetics and textiles to manufacturing and agriculture, utilize microplastics in their processes and products. This section unveils the complexities of industrial production and its contributions to microplastic pollution.

Corporate Responsibility:

We will then turn our focus to the concept of corporate responsibility. Businesses, both large and small, have the power to shape their practices, materials, and products to reduce microplastic emissions. We will delve into the strategies and initiatives that responsible corporations are adopting to address this environmental challenge.

Sustainable Solutions:

Part V shines a spotlight on sustainable solutions within the business world. We will explore innovative approaches and technologies aimed at minimizing microplastic emissions, from sustainable packaging materials to cleaner production methods. The intersection of profit and planet becomes evident as we uncover the potential for environmentally friendly practices.

Consumer Choices:

The role of consumers in influencing industry practices cannot be understated. We will investigate how consumer demand for eco-friendly products and materials is driving change within the business sector. This highlights the intricate interplay between public awareness, industry responsiveness, and market dynamics.

Regulations and Standards:

Government regulations and industry standards are instrumental in guiding corporate responsibility. We will examine the impact of legislation and industry-specific standards on business practices related to microplastic pollution, as well as the challenges and opportunities they present.

As we embark on this journey through Part V, we invite you to explore the intricate relationship between industry and the environment, the power of conscious consumer choices, and the potential for sustainable solutions. Together, we will gain insights into the transformative role that businesses and corporations can play in mitigating the microplastic predicament.

Responsibility of Manufacturers and Producers

Manufacturers and producers bear a significant responsibility in addressing microplastic pollution. In this section, we will delve into the role that these entities play in the production and distribution of products containing microplastics and explore strategies for corporate responsibility.

1. **Product Development:** Manufacturers are responsible for the development of products that contain microplastics, such as cosmetics, personal care items, and textiles. They have the power to choose alternative materials and formulations that are environmentally friendly and do not contribute to microplastic pollution.

2. **Transparency:** Transparency in product labeling is crucial. Manufacturers should provide clear information about the presence of microplastics in their products, allowing consumers to make informed choices. Transparency also extends to the disclosure of ingredients and materials used in production.

3. **Product Innovation:** Manufacturers can drive innovation in product design by exploring alternative materials and manufacturing processes that reduce or eliminate microplastics. This includes the development of biodegradable or natural alternatives to replace synthetic microplastics.

4. Sustainable Sourcing: Producers in industries like agriculture should adopt sustainable sourcing practices for products that contain microplastics, such as fertilizers and pesticides. This involves choosing materials that minimize environmental impact.

5. Recycling and Circular Economy: Manufacturers can contribute to a circular economy by designing products and packaging that are easily recyclable or reusable. This reduces the generation of microplastic waste and promotes responsible consumption.

6. Extended Producer Responsibility (EPR): EPR programs can incentivize manufacturers to take responsibility for the entire lifecycle of their products, including their end-of-life management. This encourages the adoption of more sustainable materials and practices.

7. Research and Development: Investment in research and development can lead to the creation of new materials and technologies that are less harmful to the environment. Manufacturers should prioritize R&D efforts aimed at reducing microplastic emissions.

8. Compliance with Regulations: Manufacturers must adhere to existing regulations related to microplastics and support the enforcement of these regulations. This includes following bans on certain microplastic products and ensuring compliance with labeling requirements.

9. Supply Chain Responsibility: Manufacturers should extend their commitment to corporate responsibility throughout their supply chains. This involves working with suppliers and partners to ensure sustainable practices are maintained at all levels of production.

10. **Public Engagement:** Engaging with the public and consumers to raise awareness about the responsible use of products containing microplastics is essential. Manufacturers can play a role in educating consumers about proper disposal and the environmental impact of their products.

The responsibility of manufacturers and producers extends beyond profit to encompass environmental stewardship. By adopting sustainable practices, fostering innovation, and prioritizing responsible product development, manufacturers can make significant contributions to the reduction of microplastic pollution.

Sustainable Production and Packaging Solutions

Sustainable production and packaging solutions are essential in mitigating the contribution of microplastics to environmental pollution. In this section, we will explore the strategies and innovations that businesses can adopt to reduce their environmental footprint and minimize the release of microplastics into the ecosystem.

1. **Alternative Materials:** Manufacturers and producers can transition to alternative materials that are biodegradable, compostable, or non-plastic in nature. These materials can replace traditional plastics in various applications, reducing the likeli-

hood of microplastic pollution.

2. Microplastic-Free Formulations: Companies in industries like cosmetics and personal care can reformulate their products to exclude microplastic ingredients. Natural abrasives and exfoliants, for instance, can be used instead of plastic microbeads.

3. Sustainable Packaging: Businesses should prioritize sustainable packaging solutions, such as recyclable materials, reduced packaging waste, and packaging designs that minimize the shedding of microplastics during use.

4. Biodegradable Packaging: Biodegradable packaging materials, such as bio-based plastics or compostable materials, offer environmentally friendly alternatives that break down more readily in natural environments, reducing the risk of microplastic pollution.

5. Eco-Friendly Manufacturing Practices: Adopting eco-friendly manufacturing processes that minimize microplastic emissions is crucial. This can include improved filtration systems to capture microplastics, reduced spillage during production, and responsible disposal practices.

6. Product Design for Durability: Designing products for durability and longevity can reduce the frequency of replacements and, consequently, the generation of microplastic waste.

7. Recycling and Circular Economy: Embracing a circular economy approach involves designing products and packaging for easy recycling or reuse. This reduces the demand for virgin plastics and helps minimize microplastic pollution.

8. Eco-Certifications: Obtaining eco-certifications and labels that indicate environmentally responsible practices can signal to consumers that a product or company is committed to sustainability.

9. Consumer Education: Companies can engage in consumer education campaigns to raise awareness about the environmental impact of microplastics and promote responsible product use and disposal.

10. Research and Innovation: Investment in research and innovation can lead to the development of new, sustainable materials and technologies that reduce microplastic emissions across industries.

11. Collaboration: Collaboration among businesses, industries, and stakeholders is essential to sharing best practices and driving collective efforts to address microplastic pollution. Industry associations and partnerships can play a crucial role in this regard.

Sustainable production and packaging solutions not only benefit the environment but can also enhance a company's reputation and market competitiveness.

Corporate Responsibility and CSR Initiatives

Corporate responsibility and Corporate Social Responsibility (CSR) initiatives are instrumental in addressing microplastic pollution and promoting sustainable business practices. In this section, we will explore how companies can take proactive steps to fulfill their social and environmental obligations.

1. CSR Commitment: Companies should make a commitment to corporate responsibility and integrate it into their core values and business strategies. This commitment should extend to environmental sustainability, including efforts to address microplastic pollution.

2. Environmental Impact Assessments: Conducting comprehensive assessments of the environmental impact of a company's operations is a crucial first step. This includes evaluating the potential release of microplastics and identifying areas for improvement.

3. Sustainable Supply Chains: Companies can work to ensure that their entire supply chain adheres to sustainable practices. This includes suppliers, manufacturers, distributors, and partners. Encouraging sustainable sourcing and production throughout the supply chain reduces the overall environmental footprint.

4. Product Stewardship: Adopting product stewardship principles means taking responsibility for a product's entire lifecycle, from design and production to disposal. Companies should prioritize the reduction of microplastics in products and implement take-back and recycling programs.

5. Transparency and Reporting: Transparency is essential. Companies should openly disclose their efforts, progress, and results related to microplastic reduction. Annual sustainability reports and environmental disclosures help build trust with stakeholders.

6. Engagement with Stakeholders: Engaging with various stakeholders, including customers, investors, NGOs, and communities, can provide valuable insights and feedback. Companies should actively seek input and collaborate with stakeholders on sustainability initiatives.

7. Microplastic Reduction Targets: Set clear and measurable targets for reducing microplastic emissions within the company's operations and products. These targets should align with broader sustainability goals.

8. Innovation for Sustainability: Encourage research and innovation aimed at developing alternative materials, technologies, and manufacturing processes that reduce or eliminate microplastic usage and emissions.

9. Eco-Friendly Packaging: Implement eco-friendly packaging solutions that minimize microplastic shedding and promote recycling or reuse.

10. Employee Engagement: Involve employees in sustainability initiatives by fostering a culture of environmental responsibility. Employee engagement can lead to innovative ideas and increased commitment to corporate sustainability.

11. Philanthropy and Community Engagement: Companies can support environmental causes and initiatives related to microplastic pollution through philanthropic efforts and community engagement. This includes supporting local clean-up efforts and educational programs.

12. Third-Party Certifications: Pursuing third-party certifications and endorsements related to sustainable practices can provide credibility and recognition for a company's commitment to addressing microplastic pollution.

Corporate responsibility and CSR initiatives offer a path for companies to align their operations with environmental and social objectives.

10

Local Initiatives, Education, and Activism

art VI of our exploration delves into the power of grassroots movements, community engagement, and education in the fight against microplastic pollution. In this section, we will spotlight the critical role of individuals, communities, and non-governmental organizations (NGOs) in driving change at the local level and fostering a broader understanding of the microplastic predicament.

The Local Nexus:

Our journey begins with a recognition of the local nexus—how microplastic pollution impacts communities, ecosystems, and everyday lives at the grassroots level. We will explore case studies and examples that illuminate the tangible consequences of microplastic pollution in local contexts.

Community-Led Initiatives:

We will then turn our attention to community-led initiatives and grassroots movements. Local communities, often at the forefront of environmental advocacy, are driving change through clean-up efforts, awareness campaigns, and innovative solutions. We will explore inspiring stories of community-driven microplastic reduction efforts.

Education and Awareness:

Education and awareness are fundamental pillars in addressing microplastic pollution. We will delve into the importance of environmental education in schools, community programs, and public outreach campaigns. Understanding the problem is the first step toward sustainable solutions.

Youth Engagement:

Youth activism and engagement play a significant role in advocating for environmental change. We will showcase the power of young activists and their initiatives to raise awareness, influence policy, and drive action on microplastic pollution.

Partnerships and Collaborations:

Partnerships between communities, NGOs, businesses, and governments are instrumental in scaling up local initiatives. We will explore successful collaborations that have amplified the impact of microplastic reduction efforts.

Effective Communication Strategies:

Communication strategies and advocacy techniques are essential tools in raising awareness and mobilizing communities. We will highlight effective communication campaigns and approaches used to engage the public in the fight against microplastic pollution.

As we navigate through the chapters of Part VI, we invite you to join us in celebrating the dedication of individuals and communities in addressing microplastic pollution, the transformative potential of education and awareness, and the collective strength of grassroots movements. Together, we will gain insights into the role of local initiatives, education, and activism in shaping a more sustainable future.

Citizen Movements, NGOs, and Community Projects

Citizen movements, non-governmental organizations (NGOs), and community projects are pivotal forces in addressing microplastic pollution at the local level. In this section, we will explore the transformative impact of these initiatives in mobilizing communities and driving change.

1. Grassroots Clean-Up Efforts: Citizen movements and community groups organize local clean-up campaigns to remove microplastics from beaches, rivers, and urban areas. These efforts not only reduce pollution but also raise awareness about the issue.

2. Beach and River Guardians: Many communities have established volunteer-based programs where individuals act as guardians of their local water bodies, monitoring for microplastic pollution and advocating for its reduction.

3. NGO Advocacy: Environmental NGOs play a vital role in advocating for policies and regulations aimed at reducing microplastic pollution. They conduct research, engage in public outreach, and lobby for change at local, national, and international levels.

4. Citizen Science Projects: Citizen science initiatives empower individuals to actively participate in scientific research related to microplastic pollution. These projects collect valuable data and engage communities in environmental monitoring.

5. Educational Programs: NGOs and community organizations often develop educational programs in schools and local communities to raise awareness about microplastic pollution and foster environmental stewardship among youth and adults.

6. Plastic-Free Communities: Some communities and municipalities have committed to becoming "plastic-free" by implementing bans or restrictions on single-use plastics, thereby reducing the potential sources of microplastic pollution.

7. Innovative Solutions: Community-based projects may explore innovative solutions, such as microplastic-filtering technologies in stormwater drains or sustainable packaging initiatives within local businesses.

8. Public Engagement: Engaging the public through workshops, seminars, and public events is a core strategy of NGOs and community projects. These activities inform citizens about microplastic pollution and empower them to take action.

9. Collaborations: Collaborations between citizen movements, NGOs, local governments, and businesses can amplify the impact of microplastic reduction efforts. These partnerships leverage resources, expertise, and community support.

10. Advocacy for Policy Change: Citizen movements and NGOs often advocate for policy changes at the local and national levels. They work to influence decision-makers and drive the adoption of regulations to reduce microplastic pollution.

11. Youth-Led Initiatives: Youth-led NGOs and projects are increasingly influential in raising awareness about microplastic pollution and advocating for sustainable practices. Young activists often lead the charge in driving change.

The collective efforts of citizen movements, NGOs, and community projects are instrumental in addressing microplastic pollution from the ground up. These initiatives demonstrate the power of grassroots action and community engagement in creating a more sustainable and microplastic-free future.

School Programs, Environmental Education, and Information Campaigns

School programs, environmental education, and information campaigns play a crucial role in raising awareness about microplastic pollution and fostering a sense of environmental responsibility. In this section, we will explore the impact of these initiatives on educating and mobilizing individuals and communities.

1. Environmental Curriculum: Incorporating environmental topics, including microplastic pollution, into school curricula is essential. These topics can be integrated into science, geography, and other subjects, ensuring that students are informed about the issue from an early age.

2. Hands-On Learning: Environmental education programs often include hands-on learning experiences, such as field trips to polluted areas, interactive experiments, and outdoor activities. These experiences provide a deeper understanding of microplastic pollution and its consequences.

3. School Recycling and Sustainability Projects: Schools can lead by example through recycling initiatives, reducing single-use plastics on campus, and implementing sustainability projects that engage students in addressing microplastic pollution within their school environment.

4. Guest Speakers and Workshops: Environmental experts and activists can be invited as guest speakers or workshop facilitators to educate students and teachers about microplastic pollution, its impact, and potential solutions.

5. Educational Resources: Providing educational materials and resources, such as books, videos, and online courses, can help students and educators access information about microplastic pollution and incorporate it into their learning.

6. Community Engagement: Schools can engage with the local community by organizing awareness campaigns, clean-up events, and collaboration with NGOs and community organizations focused on microplastic reduction.

7. Information Campaigns: Information campaigns within schools can raise awareness among students, parents, and staff about microplastic pollution. These campaigns may include posters, presentations, and awareness events.

8. Youth-Led Initiatives: Empowering students to take leadership roles in microplastic reduction initiatives can be highly effective. Youth-led projects within schools can drive change and inspire peers to get involved.

9. Environmental Clubs: Schools can establish environmental clubs or student organizations dedicated to addressing microplastic pollution and other environmental challenges. These clubs provide a platform for students to actively engage in environmental efforts.

10. Parent and Community Involvement: Schools can involve parents and the broader community in environmental education efforts. This collaboration extends the reach of awareness campaigns and encourages sustainable practices beyond the school gates.

11. Monitoring and Research: Schools can engage students in monitoring and research projects related to microplastic pollution in their local environments. These projects contribute valuable data and encourage a sense of ownership among students.

12. Long-Term Impact: Environmental education initiatives aim to instill a sense of responsibility and environmental stewardship in students. The long-term impact includes creating a generation of environmentally conscious individuals who actively work to reduce microplastic pollution.

By incorporating microplastic pollution awareness and education into school programs, educators and communities can play a pivotal role in shaping a more informed and environmentally responsible future generation.

Successful Communication Strategies and Partnerships

Effective communication strategies and partnerships are essential in raising awareness about microplastic pollution and mobilizing individuals and communities to take action. In this section, we will explore the strategies and collaborations that have proven successful in addressing this critical issue.

1. Clear and Accessible Messaging: Communication materials should use plain language and clear visuals to ensure that information about microplastic pollution is easily understandable by a wide audience. Avoiding technical jargon helps engage a broader audience.

2. Multi-Channel Approach: Utilizing multiple communication channels is crucial. This includes traditional media (TV, radio, newspapers), digital platforms (websites, social media, podcasts), and community events. A multi-channel approach ensures that information reaches diverse demographics.

3. Storytelling: Sharing personal stories and narratives related to microplastic pollution can be compelling. Stories humanize the issue and make it relatable to individuals, encouraging them to take action.

4. Engaging Visuals: Visual content, such as infographics, videos, and images, is highly effective in conveying information about microplastic pollution. Visuals can simplify complex concepts and capture the audience's attention.

5. Public Events and Workshops: Hosting public events, workshops, and seminars provides opportunities for face-to-face engagement. These events allow experts to share knowledge, answer questions, and build connections with the community.

6. Collaboration with Influencers: Partnering with environmental influencers, bloggers, and public figures can amplify the reach of awareness campaigns. Influencers can use their platforms to promote microplastic reduction efforts.

7. Educational Programs: Collaborating with schools and universities to integrate microplastic education into their curricula can have a lasting impact. Educational institutions are key partners in reaching and educating the next generation.

8. Partnerships with NGOs: Collaborating with environmental NGOs that specialize in microplastic pollution can provide expertise, resources, and support for awareness campaigns and initiatives.

9. Business Engagement: Engaging businesses and industries in communication efforts can promote responsible practices and reduce the use of microplastics in products and packaging.

10. Government Involvement: Partnering with local and national governments to promote policies and regulations aimed at reducing microplastic pollution is essential. Governments can support communication campaigns and provide a regulatory framework.

11. Community Partnerships: Forming partnerships with

local communities and community organizations ensures that communication efforts are tailored to the specific needs and concerns of the area.

12. Youth Engagement: Involving young activists and students in communication campaigns and initiatives can bring fresh perspectives and energy to the cause. Youth-led efforts are often highly effective in mobilizing their peers and communities.

13. Evaluation and Feedback: Continuously evaluate the impact of communication strategies and gather feedback from the audience to refine messaging and engagement methods.

Successful communication strategies and partnerships leverage the strengths of various stakeholders, from NGOs and businesses to governments and individuals, to create a unified effort in addressing microplastic pollution.

11

Technologies and Solutions

Part VII of our exploration delves into the realm of technology and innovative solutions that hold the promise of mitigating microplastic pollution. In this section, we will embark on a journey through the cutting-edge approaches, inventions, and strategies aimed at tackling this complex environmental challenge.

The Power of Innovation:

Our journey begins with a recognition of the transformative power of innovation. Human ingenuity has the potential to create solutions that can alleviate the scourge of microplastic pollution. We will explore how technology is driving progress in this crucial area.

Traditional and Modern Techniques:

We will then delve into the array of techniques and technologies, both traditional and modern, that are being harnessed to detect, collect, and manage microplastics. From filtration systems to artificial intelligence, these tools are at the forefront of the battle against microplastic pollution.

Industry-Specific Approaches:

Part VII shines a spotlight on industry-specific solutions. We will explore how various sectors, from wastewater treatment to textile production, are adopting tailored approaches to reduce microplastic emissions and implement sustainable practices.

Environmental Remediation:

Innovations in environmental remediation are critical in addressing existing microplastic pollution. We will uncover how emerging technologies are being deployed to clean up polluted environments and restore ecosystems.

Cross-Disciplinary Collaboration:

Part VII emphasizes the importance of cross-disciplinary collaboration. Scientists, engineers, environmentalists, and policymakers are working together to develop holistic solutions that encompass technology, policy, and public engagement.

Challenges and Future Prospects:

Our exploration will conclude by examining the challenges that lie ahead and the future prospects for solving the microplastic predicament. The path forward requires continued innovation, global cooperation, and unwavering commitment.

As we embark on this journey through Part VII, we invite you to witness the exciting frontier of technology and solutions in the fight against microplastic pollution. Together, we will gain insights into the potential for innovative approaches to shape a cleaner and more sustainable future.

Traditional and New Technologies for Microplastic Removal

The removal of microplastics from the environment is a critical step in mitigating their harmful effects. In this section, we will explore both traditional and cutting-edge technologies that are used to detect and remove microplastics from various settings, including water bodies and ecosystems.

1. Filtration Systems: Traditional filtration systems, such as sand and mesh filters, are used to physically capture microplastics from wastewater, stormwater, and industrial effluents. These systems are effective at trapping larger microplastics.

2. Membrane Filtration: Membrane filtration technologies, including microfiltration and ultrafiltration membranes, are employed in water treatment plants to remove microplastics, even those as small as nanometers in size.

3. Electrocoagulation: Electrocoagulation involves the use of electrical charges to destabilize and clump microplastics together, making them easier to remove through sedimentation or filtration.

4. Magnetic Separation: Magnetic separation techniques can target magnetic microplastics by applying magnetic fields to separate them from other materials in water or sediment.

5. Chemical Precipitation: Chemical precipitation methods involve adding coagulants or flocculants to water to bind microplastics, forming larger particles that can be removed through settling or filtration.

6. Autonomous Underwater Vehicles (AUVs): AUVs equipped with sensors and cameras are used to survey and identify microplastic pollution in marine environments. These vehicles can provide valuable data for research and monitoring.

7. Remote Sensing: Remote sensing technologies, such as satellites and drones, are used to detect and map areas of microplastic pollution in oceans and water bodies, aiding in the assessment of the extent of the problem.

8. Nanotechnology: Nanotechnology-based solutions are being explored to capture and remove microplastics at the nanoscale. Nanomaterials with high adsorption capacities are under development for this purpose.

9. Microbial Degradation: Researchers are investigating microbial degradation as a natural method to break down microplastics in the environment. Certain microorganisms have the ability to enzymatically degrade plastics.

10. Microplastic-Collecting Booms: Floating booms equipped with nets or other collection devices are deployed in rivers and water bodies to capture floating microplastics before they enter oceans or other ecosystems.

11. Benthic Sleds and Sediment Sampling: Specialized equipment like benthic sleds and sediment samplers are used to collect samples from the seafloor, allowing researchers to study microplastic pollution in marine sediments.

12. Biofilters and Green Infrastructure: Biofilters and green infrastructure solutions in urban areas help capture microplastics from stormwater runoff, preventing their entry into water bodies.

13. Innovative Materials: Researchers are exploring the use of innovative materials, such as sponge-like structures and aerogels, to capture microplastics efficiently from water sources.

14. Ocean Cleanup Initiatives: Innovative ocean cleanup projects, such as the deployment of passive drifting systems, aim to collect and remove large amounts of plastic debris and microplastics from the oceans.

15. Public Participation: Crowdsourcing and citizen science initiatives often use mobile apps and online platforms to engage the public in microplastic monitoring and data collection.

These technologies, both traditional and cutting-edge, play a crucial role in detecting and removing microplastics from various environments. Their effectiveness depends on factors such as the type of microplastics, the size of particles, and the specific setting in which they are deployed. Continued research and innovation in this field are essential to developing more efficient and sustainable microplastic removal methods.

Innovations in Industry and Research

Innovations in both industry and research are instrumental in addressing microplastic pollution and developing sustainable practices. In this section, we will explore the latest advancements and breakthroughs that are contributing to the reduction of microplastics in various sectors.

1. Microplastic-Free Products: Industries are innovating to develop products that are entirely free of microplastics. This includes cosmetics, personal care items, and cleaning products that use natural, biodegradable, or alternative materials in place of microplastics.

2. Biodegradable Polymers: Researchers and industries are exploring biodegradable polymers as alternatives to traditional plastics. These materials break down more readily in the environment, reducing the persistence of microplastics.

3. Sustainable Textiles: The textile industry is adopting sustainable practices, including the use of recycled fibers and reduced shedding fabrics, to minimize microplastic emissions from clothing.

4. Eco-Friendly Packaging: Innovations in packaging materials focus on reducing the shedding of microplastics and promoting recyclability and reusability.

5. Microfiber Filtration: Washing machine manufacturers are developing built-in microfiber filtration systems that capture microfibers released during laundry cycles, preventing them from entering wastewater.

6. Green Chemistry: The field of green chemistry explores environmentally friendly chemical processes and materials that minimize the generation of microplastics in industrial processes.

7. Microplastic Detection Tools: Researchers are developing advanced tools and analytical techniques, such as Raman spectroscopy and FTIR microscopy, to more accurately detect and analyze microplastics in various environments.

8. Nanotechnology Solutions: Nanotechnology is being employed to design nanoscale materials that can efficiently capture and remove microplastics from water sources.

9. Improved Water Treatment: Innovations in water treatment technologies aim to enhance the removal of microplastics from wastewater, ensuring that fewer microplastics are released into the environment.

10. Circular Economy Initiatives: Industries are embracing circular economy principles, designing products and processes that reduce waste and minimize the generation of microplastic pollution.

11. Sustainable Fishing Gear: The fishing industry is exploring the use of eco-friendly fishing gear, including alternatives to synthetic nets and lines that shed microplastics into the oceans.

12. Ocean Cleanup Technologies: Innovations in ocean cleanup technologies, such as autonomous drones and passive collection systems, are being deployed to remove macroplastics and microplastics from marine environments.

13. Research Collaboration: Collaboration between researchers, industries, and governments fosters the development of innovative solutions and the sharing of knowledge to combat microplastic pollution.

14. Bio-Based Materials: The development of bio-based materials and polymers derived from renewable sources is reducing reliance on traditional plastics, contributing to microplastic reduction.

15. Sustainable Agriculture: Agriculture practices are evolving to incorporate sustainable methods that minimize microplastic contamination in soil and water through reduced plastic mulch usage and responsible fertilizer application.

These innovations in both industry and research are driving progress toward the reduction of microplastic pollution and the development of sustainable alternatives. They demonstrate the commitment of various sectors to address the environmental challenges posed by microplastics and pave the way for a cleaner and more sustainable future.

Industry-Specific Approaches and Best Practices

Different industries have unique challenges and opportunities when it comes to addressing microplastic pollution. In this section, we will explore industry-specific approaches and best practices that are being adopted to reduce microplastics in various sectors.

1. Cosmetics and Personal Care Products:

- Shift to Microplastic-Free Ingredients: Many companies in the cosmetics and personal care industry are transitioning to microplastic-free ingredients, replacing microbeads and microplastics with natural alternatives like bamboo or rice powders.
- Transparency and Labeling: Brands are increasingly transparent about the ingredients used in their products, helping consumers make informed choices and avoid products containing microplastics.

2. Textile and Fashion Industry:

- Sustainable Fabrics: Innovations in textiles include the development of fabrics that shed fewer microfibers during washing, as well as the use of sustainable materials like organic cotton and recycled fibers.
- Washing Machine Filtration: Some washing machine manufacturers are incorporating microfiber filtration systems to capture microfibers released during laundry cycles.
- Consumer Education: Brands are educating consumers on proper garment care and the use of microfiber-catching laundry bags to reduce microfiber emissions.

3. Packaging Industry:

- Eco-Friendly Materials: Companies are exploring eco-friendly packaging materials that minimize microplastic shedding and promote recycling or reuse.
- Packaging Design: Innovative packaging designs focus on reducing waste and preventing microplastic contamination during product use.

4. Fishing Industry:

- Sustainable Gear: Sustainable fishing practices involve using gear that minimizes the release of microplastics into the oceans. This includes using biodegradable fishing nets and lines.
- Proper Gear Disposal: Initiatives encourage responsible disposal of fishing gear to prevent abandoned or lost gear from contributing to microplastic pollution.

5. Agriculture:

- Reduced Plastic Mulch: Agricultural practices are shifting towards reduced use of plastic mulch in favor of biodegradable alternatives or no-till farming methods that reduce soil erosion and microplastic contamination.
- Responsible Fertilizer Application: Precision agriculture techniques are employed to minimize the spread of microplastics from fertilizers into soil and water.

6. Food and Beverage Industry:

- Packaging Choices: Food and beverage companies are selecting packaging options that minimize the release of microplastics, such as avoiding plastic tea bags or using non-plastic alternatives.
- Sustainable Sourcing: Sourcing practices that prioritize environmentally friendly materials and processes help reduce microplastic contamination in food products.

7. Wastewater Treatment:

- Advanced Filtration: Wastewater treatment plants are adopting advanced filtration systems and technologies to effectively capture microplastics before treated water is released into the environment.
- Monitoring and Research: Continuous monitoring and research are conducted to improve the efficiency of microplastic removal in wastewater treatment processes.

8. Electronics and Technology:

- Eco-Design: Electronics manufacturers are incorporating eco-design principles to reduce the use of plastics and microplastics in their products and packaging.
- E-Waste Recycling: Proper recycling and disposal of electronic waste help prevent the release of microplastics from deteriorating electronic components.

9. Healthcare and Medical Devices:

- Microplastic-Free Medical Products: The medical industry is working to develop microplastic-free medical products and packaging materials to minimize the introduction of microplastics into the healthcare environment.

Future Challenges and Perspectives

While significant progress has been made in addressing microplastic pollution, there remain several challenges and uncertainties on the horizon. In this section, we will explore the future challenges and perspectives related to microplastic pollution.

1.   **Emerging Microplastics:** As new types of plastics and microplastics continue to enter the market, researchers and policymakers must stay vigilant to identify and assess their potential environmental impacts.

2. **Microplastics in Soil:** Understanding and mitigating microplastic pollution in terrestrial environments, including agricultural soils, is an emerging challenge that requires further research and solutions.

3. **Ecological Impacts:** The long-term ecological consequences of microplastic pollution on ecosystems and biodiversity are not fully understood. Ongoing research is needed to assess and mitigate these impacts.

4. **Human Health Concerns:** Research into the potential health effects of microplastic exposure in humans is ongoing. Future studies will help determine the extent of health risks associated with microplastic ingestion and inhalation.

5. **Regulatory Frameworks:** The development and implementation of comprehensive regulatory frameworks at national and international levels are crucial to address microplastic pollution effectively. Harmonizing regulations and enforcement mechanisms is a challenge.

6. **Circular Economy Transition:** Achieving a circular economy, where plastics are recycled, reused, or replaced with sustainable alternatives, is essential for reducing the generation of microplastics. This transition poses challenges in terms of infrastructure, technology, and consumer behavior.

7. Global Cooperation: Microplastic pollution is a global issue that requires collaboration among nations, organizations, and industries. Building consensus and cooperation on a global scale can be challenging but is necessary for meaningful change.

8. Public Awareness and Education: Sustaining public awareness and education efforts is essential for long-term behavioral change and consumer choices that reduce microplastic pollution.

9. Technological Innovation: Continued innovation in microplastic detection, removal, and sustainable materials is crucial to develop more effective solutions.

10. Data and Monitoring: Comprehensive and standardized data collection and monitoring efforts are needed to assess the extent of microplastic pollution, track trends, and evaluate the effectiveness of mitigation measures.

11. Environmental Justice: Addressing microplastic pollution should include considerations of environmental justice, ensuring that vulnerable communities do not bear a disproportionate burden of its impacts.

12. Interdisciplinary Research: Collaborative research that bridges multiple disciplines, from environmental science to public health and policy, is vital for gaining a holistic understanding of microplastic pollution.

While these challenges are significant, they also present opportunities for innovation, collaboration, and positive change.

Technological Developments and Research Gaps

In the ongoing battle against microplastic pollution, technological developments and research are at the forefront of efforts to better understand, detect, and mitigate this environmental threat. In this section, we will delve into the evolving technological landscape and the research gaps that warrant further exploration.

1. Improved Detection Technologies:

- Advanced Microscopy: Continued advancements in microscopy techniques, including scanning electron microscopy (SEM) and transmission electron microscopy (TEM), allow for more precise identification and quantification of microplastics.
- Spectroscopy Methods: Spectroscopic techniques such as Raman and FTIR spectroscopy are being refined to enhance the accuracy and speed of microplastic analysis.
- Autonomous Sensors: Development of autonomous sensors and monitoring systems that can detect and report microplastics in real-time is a promising avenue of research.

2. Source Attribution Technology:

- Tracing Origins: Developing methods to trace the sources and pathways of microplastics in the environment is crucial. This includes chemical markers and isotopic analysis to determine the origins of microplastics.

3. Risk Assessment Models:

- Ecological Models: Building comprehensive ecological models to assess the impact of microplastic pollution on ecosystems and species is an ongoing research challenge. These models can help predict long-term effects.
- Human Health Models: Developing models to evaluate the potential health risks associated with microplastic exposure in humans is essential for risk assessment.

4. Microplastic Removal Technologies:

- Efficient Removal Methods: Research is needed to improve the efficiency of microplastic removal technologies, such as advanced filtration systems and nano-material-based sorbents.
- Environmental Remediation: Innovations in environmental remediation methods to clean up polluted areas and sediments require further exploration.

5. Standardized Sampling Protocols:

- Standardization of sampling protocols across different environments, including water bodies, sediments, soils, and air, is necessary for accurate comparisons and assessments.

6. Fate and Transport Studies:

- Understanding the fate and transport of microplastics in various environments, including oceans, rivers, and atmospheric transport, requires further research to inform pollution prevention strategies.

7. Risk Assessment for Human Health:

- Comprehensive studies on the potential health risks associated with microplastic ingestion and inhalation are essential for informing public health policies and guidelines.

8. Biodegradable Alternatives:

- Research into the development and performance of biodegradable plastics and materials that do not contribute to microplastic pollution is ongoing.

9. Circular Economy Solutions:

- Innovations in the design of products, packaging, and recycling processes that promote a circular economy and reduce microplastic generation are areas of active research.

10. Collaboration Across Disciplines: - Fostering interdisciplinary collaboration between environmental scientists, chemists, engineers, and health professionals is crucial for holistic research on microplastic pollution.

11. Public Engagement and Behavioral Research: - Understanding human behaviors and perceptions related to microplastic pollution is vital for developing effective public engagement strategies.

12. Regulatory Frameworks: - Research on the development and evaluation of regulatory frameworks and policies for microplastic management and reduction is essential.

13. Environmental Justice: - Research on the disproportionate impacts of microplastic pollution on marginalized and vulnerable communities is needed to address environmental justice concerns.

14. Long-Term Monitoring: - Establishing long-term monitoring programs to track changes in microplastic pollution levels and assess the effectiveness of mitigation measures is essential.

Recommendations for Policymakers and Industry

Effective strategies to combat microplastic pollution require collaboration between policymakers, industries, and other stakeholders. In this section, we provide recommendations for policymakers and industry leaders to address the challenges posed by microplastic pollution.

Policymakers:

1. **Establish Comprehensive Regulations:** Develop and implement comprehensive regulations that address the production, use, and disposal of microplastics across industries. This includes bans or restrictions on certain types of microplastics in consumer products.
2. **Support Research:** Allocate funding for research on the environmental and health impacts of microplastics, as well as the development of innovative detection and removal technologies.
3. **Promote Circular Economy:** Encourage industries to adopt

circular economy principles, emphasizing recycling, reuse, and sustainable design to minimize microplastic generation.

4. **Implement Monitoring Programs:** Establish and maintain robust monitoring programs to track microplastic levels in various environments, providing data for informed decision-making.

5. **Support Public Awareness:** Invest in public awareness campaigns to educate citizens about microplastic pollution, its impacts, and actions they can take to reduce their microplastic footprint.

6. **Encourage Collaboration:** Foster collaboration among governments, industries, NGOs, and research institutions to develop coordinated strategies for addressing microplastic pollution on a global scale.

7. **Incentivize Sustainable Practices:** Provide incentives, such as tax breaks or subsidies, for businesses that adopt sustainable practices and reduce their use of microplastics.

8. **Promote Eco-Friendly Alternatives:** Promote research and development of eco-friendly alternatives to microplastics and support industries in transitioning to these alternatives.

Industry Leaders:

1. **Phase Out Microplastics:** Commit to phasing out the use of microplastics in products, particularly in cosmetics, personal care items, cleaning products, and packaging materials.

2. **Invest in Research:** Invest in research and development to find innovative alternatives to microplastics and improve

product formulations to reduce microplastic shedding.

3. **Improve Transparency:** Be transparent about product ingredients, particularly the presence or absence of microplastics, to empower consumers to make informed choices.

4. **Adopt Sustainable Packaging:** Embrace sustainable packaging materials and designs that minimize microplastic shedding and promote recycling and reusability.

5. **Support Recycling Initiatives:** Support and invest in recycling programs that aim to reduce plastic waste and prevent the fragmentation of plastics into microplastics.

6. **Collaborate for Solutions:** Collaborate with other businesses, researchers, and government bodies to develop industry-wide best practices and solutions for microplastic pollution.

7. **Engage in Responsible Disposal:** Ensure responsible disposal of waste products and materials to prevent microplastics from entering the environment.

8. **Prioritize Environmental Impact:** Integrate environmental impact assessments into product development and life cycle analysis to minimize microplastic emissions.

9. **Educate Employees:** Educate employees about the importance of microplastic pollution mitigation and involve them in sustainable practices within the organization.

10. **Engage in Advocacy:** Advocate for supportive policies and regulations at the local, national, and international levels to address microplastic pollution.

By taking these recommendations into account, policymakers and industry leaders can work together to reduce the presence of microplastics in the environment, protect ecosystems and human health, and move toward a more sustainable future.

12

Final Words

As we embarked on the journey through the pages of this book, "Micro Plastic: Mega Consequences," my aim was not only to raise awareness about the far-reaching impacts of microplastics but also to present tangible solutions and approaches to aid us on the path to a more sustainable future.

It's a journey that has taken us from the tiniest particles in our oceans to the global tables of political decision-making, all with the intention of deepening our understanding of the urgency and complexity of this issue.

However, our journey does not end here. The challenge of tackling microplastic pollution is dynamic and requires our continuous attention and commitment. It is my sincere hope that this book serves not just as a source of information, but also as a call to action. Each of us has the power to effect change – whether through conscious choices in our daily lives, involvement in community projects, or by driving political initiatives.

In that spirit, I encourage you to continue your journey and remain committed to our planet and its inhabitants. If you wish to further explore the intricate interplay of our times, I recommend my other works: "Unveiling Shadows: Navigating Centuries of Controversies," which delves into the hidden sides of history and their impact on the modern world, and "Microstate to Macro-Consequences: Environmental Paradoxes," shedding light on the unexpected and often overlooked ecological challenges of our era.

Thank you for joining me on this journey, and I hope we can take the next steps towards a brighter, more sustainable future together.

With gratitude and hope,

Sophia Fairview